# The Mediterranean Diet Cookbook

## 90 Delicious and Nutritious Recipes for a Healthier Lifestyle

### Juanita T. Williams

# Table of Contents

# Introduction

As the sun rose over the Mediterranean Sea, Maria sat at her kitchen table and began her day with a cup of strong, black coffee and a bowl of olives, tomatoes, and feta cheese. She had been following the Mediterranean diet for several months, and she had already noticed several positive changes in her health and well-being.

Maria had always struggled with her weight and had been diagnosed with high blood pressure and high cholesterol. Despite trying various diets and exercise programs, she had been unable to make lasting changes to her health. That is until she discovered the Mediterranean diet.

At first, Maria was skeptical. How could a diet based on the foods she had always enjoyed fresh vegetables, fruits, nuts, whole grains, and olive oil be so effective in improving her health? But she decided to give it a try, and she was amazed by the results.

As she followed the diet, Maria began to lose weight and her blood pressure and cholesterol levels improved. She had more energy and felt more alert and focused throughout the day. She even noticed a difference in her skin, which looked brighter and more radiant.

Maria was thrilled with the changes she was experiencing and was grateful for the opportunity to improve her health through the foods she loved. She knew that the Mediterranean diet was more than just a fad or a quick fix, it was a way of life that had the power to transform her health and well-being.

The Mediterranean Diet, also known as the Mediterranean lifestyle, is a way of eating that has been around for centuries, originating from the countries around the Mediterranean Sea. This diet is based on the traditional diets of the countries that surround the Mediterranean, such as Greece, Italy, Spain, and Turkey.

It is characterized by the high consumption of fruits, vegetables, whole grains, legumes, nuts, and olive oil while limiting the consumption of red meat, processed foods, and saturated fats. Additionally, it also emphasizes the importance of consuming fish, poultry, and dairy products in moderation.

The Mediterranean Diet has been celebrated for its beneficial effects on physical and mental health and has been recommended for its role in the prevention and management of numerous chronic diseases. It is also praised for its focus on the enjoyment of food and social gatherings, as well as its potential to promote a healthy lifestyle.

The Mediterranean Diet is a unique way of eating that is rooted in centuries-old traditions, offering a healthful and delicious approach to food. It encourages people to make healthier food choices while also allowing them to enjoy meals with family and friends.

With its emphasis on fresh and seasonal ingredients, the Mediterranean Diet has been recognized by health experts as one of the most nutritious and healthful diets in the world. With its focus on the enjoyment of food, it is a diet that can be enjoyed for a lifetime.

For centuries, people around the world have enjoyed the delicious flavors of the Mediterranean region. With its rich history and culture, the Mediterranean Diet has become one of the healthiest dietary patterns in the world. From olive oil to fresh vegetables and legumes, there is something for everyone to enjoy.

The Diet is rich in vegetables, fruits, nuts, whole grains, legumes, and healthy fats. The diet also includes fish, poultry, eggs, and dairy products, but limits red meat and sweets.

There are numerous health benefits associated with the Diet. Studies have shown that it can reduce the risk of heart disease, stroke, type 2 diabetes, certain types of cancer, and obesity. It can also help to reduce inflammation, improve blood pressure, and improve cholesterol levels. It has also been shown to reduce the risk of age-related cognitive decline and improve overall health and well-being.

The Mediterranean Diet is also rich in antioxidants and polyphenols, which are powerful compounds that can help protect the body from oxidative stress and chronic diseases. Additionally, the diet is rich in fiber, which can help improve digestion and weight management.

When following the Diet, it is important to focus on eating whole, unprocessed foods. This includes fresh fruits and vegetables, whole grains, legumes, nuts, seeds, and healthy fats. It is also important to limit red meat, processed meats, and sweets.

In addition to eating healthy foods, the Diet also emphasizes physical activity. Which entails cycling, walking, running, swimming, and other forms of exercise. Incorporating physical activity into your daily routine can help to improve your overall health and well-being.

The Diet is a great way to enjoy delicious and nutritious food while maintaining a healthy lifestyle. So, if you're looking for a delicious and healthy way to eat, give the Mediterranean Diet a try!

# Chapter 1

## Benefits of the Mediterranean Diet

The Mediterranean diet is a dietary pattern that is based on the traditional foods that are consumed in countries around the Mediterranean Sea, such as Italy, Greece, and Spain. This diet is high in vegetables, fruits, nuts, whole grains, legumes, and olive oil, and it also includes moderate amounts of fish, poultry, and wine. It is low in red meat, processed meats, and added sugars.

There are many potential health benefits associated with following a Mediterranean diet. Here are a few:

- **Weight loss**: Several studies have found that the Mediterranean diet can be effective for weight loss. This may be due in part to the fact that the diet is high in fiber and low in added sugars, which can help to reduce calorie intake and promote weight loss.

- **Heart health**: The Mediterranean diet is beneficial for heart health in several ways. It can lower blood pressure, reduce levels of

LDL ("bad") cholesterol, and reduce the risk of heart disease.

- **Diabetes management**: The Mediterranean diet has also been found to help manage type 2 diabetes. It can improve blood sugar control, reduce the need for diabetes medications, and reduce the risk of complications associated with diabetes.

- **Cognitive function**: Some research suggests that the Mediterranean diet may have a protective effect on cognitive function, including memory and thinking skills.

- **Cancer prevention**: Some studies have found that the Mediterranean diet may reduce the risk of certain types of cancer, including breast, colon, and prostate cancer.

Overall, the Mediterranean diet is a healthy and balanced eating pattern that can provide several benefits for overall health and well-being.

# Chapter 2

## Recipes for Breakfast

**1. Greek Yogurt Parfait**

**Ingredients include:** Greek yogurt

-Recent berries

-Nuts\s-Honey

**Preparation:**

1. In a mixing bowl, combine Greek yogurt, fresh berries, and nuts.

2. Drizzle with honey on top.

3. Enjoy.

**2. Mediterranean Frittata**

**Ingredients include:** Olive oil, onion, red bell pepper, garlic, spinach, eggs

-Salt and pepper -Feta cheese

**Preparation**:

1. Preheat the oven to 375°F.

2. Melt the butter in a large ovenproof skillet over medium heat.

3. Cook until the onion and bell pepper are softened.

4. Cook for an additional minute after adding the garlic and spinach.

5. Whisk together the eggs, feta cheese, salt, and pepper in a mixing bowl.

6. Pour in the egg mixture and cook until the edges are set.

7. Place skillet in oven and bake for 8-10 minutes.

8. Cut into wedges to serve.

3. **Poached Egg on Avocado Toast**

**Ingredients include**: Avocado, whole wheat bread, egg, and lemon juice

-Pepper and salt

**Preparation**:

1. Toast 1 slice of whole wheat bread.

2. Mash the avocado and spread it on the toast.

3. Cook the egg to the desired doneness.

4. Arrange a poached egg on top of the avocado toast.

5. Season with salt and pepper and drizzle with lemon juice.

6. Enjoy.

## 4. Mediterranean Egg Sandwich

**Ingredients include**: Whole wheat bread -Egg -Tomato -Cucumber -Feta cheese -Olive oil -Salt and pepper

**Preparation**:

1. Toast 1 slice of whole wheat bread.

2. Cook an egg to the desired doneness.

3. Assemble the sandwich by layering it with tomato, cucumber, feta cheese, an egg, and olive oil.

4. Season with salt and pepper to taste.

5. Enjoy.


## 5. Scrambled Eggs and Vegetables

**Ingredients include**: Olive oil -Onion -Red bell pepper

-Garlic\s-Spinach\&-Eggs

-Salt and pepper -Feta cheese

**Preparation**:

1. In a large skillet over medium heat, heat up olive oil.

2. Cook until the onion and bell pepper are softened.

3. Cook for an additional minute after adding the garlic and spinach.

4. Scramble the eggs in the skillet until they are cooked through.

5. Season with salt and pepper and top with feta cheese.

6. Serve.

## 6. Mediterranean Omelet

**Ingredients include**: Olive oil, onion, red bell pepper, garlic

-Spinach\s-Eggs

-Salt and pepper -Feta cheese

**Preparation**:

1. In a large skillet over medium heat, heat up olive oil.

2. Cook until the onion and bell pepper are softened.

3. Cook for an additional minute after adding the garlic and spinach.

4. Combine eggs, feta cheese, salt, and pepper in a mixing bowl.

5. Pour in the egg mixture and cook until the edges are set.

6. Fold the omelet in half and cook for another minute.

7. Serve.

### 7. **Breakfast Wraps from the Mediterranean**

**Ingredients include**: Whole wheat tortillas, eggs, tomato, cucumber, feta cheese, olive oil, salt, and pepper

**Preparation**:

1. Preheat a skillet on medium heat.

2. Scramble the eggs in the skillet until they are cooked through.

3. Fill tortillas with scrambled eggs, tomato, cucumber, feta cheese, and olive oil.

4. Season with salt and pepper to taste.

5. Enjoy.

## 8. Mediterranean Quinoa Breakfast Bowl

**Ingredients include:**

-Olive oil

-Onion

-Red bell pepper

-Garlic

-Spinach

-Eggs

-Salt and pepper

-Feta cheese

**Preparation:**

1. Prepare the quinoa according to the package directions.

2. In a large skillet over medium heat, heat up olive oil.

3. Cook until the onion and bell pepper are softened.

4. Cook for an additional minute after adding the garlic and spinach.

5. Scramble the eggs in the skillet until they are cooked through.

6. Stir in the cooked quinoa in the skillet.

7. Season with salt and pepper and top with feta cheese.

8. Serve.


9. **Mediterranean Toast**

**Ingredients include:**

-Whole wheat bread

-Tomato -Cucumber

-Olive oil

-Salt and pepper

-Feta cheese

**Preparation:**

1. Toast 1 slice of whole wheat bread.

2. Spread tomato, cucumber, feta cheese, and olive oil on toast.

3. Season with salt and pepper to taste.

4. Enjoy.

10. **Shakshuka**

**Ingredients include**:

-Olive oil -Onion

-Red bell pepper -Garlic

-Tomatoes\s-Eggs

-Salt and pepper -Feta cheese

**Preparation**:

1. In a large skillet over medium heat, heat up olive oil.

2. Cook until the onion and bell pepper are softened.

3. Cook for an additional minute after adding the garlic.

4. Cook until the tomatoes are softened.

5. Create wells in the tomato mixture and crack the eggs into them.

6. Cook, covered until eggs are cooked to the desired doneness.

7. Top with feta cheese and season with salt and pepper.

8. Serve.

# Chapter 3

## Appetizers and small snacks

**1. Greek Feta and Olive Bites**

**Preparation**- Spread feta cheese on whole-wheat crackers and top with a pitted kalamata olive and oregano.

**2. Marinated Grilled Vegetables**

**Preparation**- Combine olive oil, garlic, oregano, lemon juice, and sea salt in a bowl and marinate zucchini, eggplant, and bell peppers. Grill until vegetables are soft.

### 3. **Hummus with Pita Chips**

**Preparation**- In a food processor, combine cooked chickpeas, tahini, lemon juice, garlic, and water until smooth. Serve with pita chips cooked from scratch.

### 4. **Mediterranean Antipasto Platter**

**Preparation**- On a platter, arrange olives, roasted peppers, artichoke hearts, fresh mozzarella, roasted eggplant, and prosciutto.

### 5. **Fried Eggplant and Feta**

**Preparation**- Cut eggplant into thin slices, dip it in egg and breadcrumbs, and fry until golden in olive oil.

Crumbled feta and minced parsley on top.

6. **Baked Feta**

**Preparation**- In an oven-safe dish, layer feta cheese with chopped tomatoes, oregano, and olive oil. Bake for 20 minutes, or until the cheese melts.

7. **Roasted Red Pepper and Feta Dip**

**Preparation**- In a food processor, combine the roasted red peppers, feta cheese, cream cheese, garlic, and olive oil until smooth. Serve alongside whole-wheat pita chips.

8. **Greek Salad Skewers**

**Preparation**- Thread skewers with cucumber, tomato, feta cheese, kalamata olives, and oregano. Drizzle with lemon juice and olive oil.

9. **Grilled Halloumi with Mint**

**Preparation**- Brush slices of halloumi cheese with olive oil and grill until lightly golden. Serve with fresh mint and a squeeze of lemon on top.

10. Toss roasted chickpeas with olive oil, smoked paprika, cumin, and sea salt. 25 minutes, or until golden and crispy.

11. **Pita with Spinach and Feta**
**Preparation**- Toast whole-wheat pita bread and top with wilted spinach, feta cheese, and olive oil.

12. **Eggplant-Yogurt Dip**
**Preparation-In** a food processor, combine the roasted eggplant, plain yogurt, garlic, mint, and olive oil until smooth. Serve alongside whole-wheat pita chips.

13. **Mediterranean-style kebab**
**Preparation**- Skewer cubed chicken, bell peppers, tomatoes, onions, and mushrooms. Marinate in an olive oil, lemon juice, and oregano combination. Grill until well cooked.

## 14. **Baked Olives**

**Preparation**- Place a variety of olives on a baking sheet. Drizzle with olive oil and bake for 15 minutes, or until well warmed.

## 15. **Fava Bean Dip**

**Preparation**- In a food processor, combine cooked fava beans, garlic, lemon juice, and olive oil until smooth. Serve with vegetables or whole-wheat pita chips.

# Chapter 4

## Recipes for the Main Course Dishes

**1. Greek Lemon Chicken**

Preparation- Season the chicken with olive oil, garlic powder, salt, and pepper. Cook until golden brown on the grill or in the oven. Before serving, squeeze lemon juice over the chicken.

**2. Grilled Fish with Vegetables**

**Preparation**- Rub white fish with olive oil, garlic, salt, and pepper before grilling. Grill until well cooked.

Serve with grilled vegetables on the side.

3. **Italian Stuffed Peppers**

**Preparation**- Stuff cooked rice, ground beef, Italian seasoning, and Parmesan cheese into bell peppers. Bake until the peppers are soft.

4. **Greek Salad**

**Preparation**- Combine lettuce, tomatoes, cucumbers, feta cheese, Kalamata olives, and olive oil in a mixing bowl.

5. **Mediterranean Lasagna**

**Preparation**- Combine cooked lasagna noodles, ricotta cheese, spinach, and Italian herbs. Marinara sauce and cheese on top.

## 6. Eggplant Parmesan

**Preparation**- Season eggplant rounds with olive oil, salt, and pepper. Grill or bake till golden brown. Marinara sauce and cheese should be layered on top.

## 7. Seared Salmon with Zucchini

**Preparation**- Season the salmon with salt and pepper. Cook until done in a pan. Serve with sautéed zucchini on the side.

## 8. **Mediterranean Chicken Wrap**

**Preparation**: On a flatbread wrap, layer cooked chicken, feta cheese, tomatoes, and lettuce. Season with salt and pepper and drizzle with olive oil.

## 9. **Roasted Vegetable Salad**

**Preparation**- Toss tomatoes, red peppers, eggplant, and zucchini together. Roast till gently browned in the oven. Serve with olive oil and balsamic vinegar on a bed of lettuce.

## 10. **Greek-style rice**

**Preparation**- Cook white rice with garlic, oregano, and feta cheese. Serve with grilled chicken or fish on the side.

## 11. **Hummus and Pita**

**Preparation**- Spread hummus on whole wheat pita bread. Serve with chopped tomatoes and cucumbers on top.

## 12. **Greek Moussaka**

**Preparation**- Layer cooked eggplant with ground beef, tomato, and spice mixture. Bake until golden brown and topped with a creamy béchamel sauce.

**13. Platter of Grilled Vegetables:**
**Preparation**- Grill eggplant, zucchini, and red peppers. Serve with hummus on the side.

**14. Spinach Pie**
**Preparation**- Combine chopped spinach, feta cheese, and ricotta cheese in a mixing bowl. Roll out a sheet of puff pastry and place the spinach mixture on top. Cook till golden brown.

**15. Greek Pastitsio**
**Preparation**- Layer-cooked macaroni noodles with ground beef, tomato, and spice mixture. Bake until golden

brown and topped with a creamy béchamel sauce.

## 16. Stuffed Tomatoes

**Preparation**- Stuff cooked quinoa, feta cheese, and black olives into tomato halves. Bake until the tomatoes are soft.

## 17. Baked White Fish in the Mediterranean Style

**Preparation**- Rub white fish with olive oil, garlic, and Italian herbs. Bake until well done.

## 18. Grilled Eggplant with Feta:

**Preparation**- Slice eggplant into rounds, season with olive oil, salt, and pepper, and grill. Grill till golden brown. Serve with feta cheese and a sprinkle of olive oil on top.

19. Greek-Style Skewer cubes of chicken and veggies for souvlaki. Grill until well cooked. Serve with tzatziki sauce on the side.

20. **Mediterranean-Style Pizza Preparation-** Combine diced tomatoes, black olives, feta cheese, and oregano on a pre-made pizza crust. Cook till golden brown.

# Chapter 5

## Vegetable Recipes

1. **Mediterranean Roasted Vegetables**

**Ingredients include-** eggplant, zucchini, red peppers, red onion, garlic, olive oil, oregano, thyme, salt, and pepper.

**Preparation**: Heat the oven to 400°F. Make small cubes of eggplant, zucchini, and red pepper. Toss with chopped red onion, minced garlic, olive oil, oregano, thyme, salt, and pepper on a baking sheet. Roast the vegetables for 20-25 minutes, or until soft and gently browned.

## 2. **Mediterranean Orzo Salad**

**Ingredients include**- orzo, cherry tomatoes, cucumber, olives, feta cheese, red onion, parsley, lemon juice, olive oil, salt, and pepper.

**Preparation**: Cook the orzo according to the package directions. To cool, drain and rinse with cold water. Combine cooked orzo, cherry tomatoes, cucumber, olives, feta cheese, red onion, parsley, lemon juice, olive oil, salt, and pepper in a large mixing bowl. Place in the refrigerator until ready to serve.

3. **Mediterranean Stuffed Peppers**

**Ingredients include**- bell peppers, quinoa, artichoke hearts, spinach, mushrooms, feta cheese, olive oil, garlic, oregano, salt, and pepper.

**Preparation**: Heat the oven to 350°F. Remove the seeds from the bell peppers and cut them in half. Cook the quinoa according to the package directions. Combine cooked quinoa, artichoke hearts, spinach, mushrooms, feta cheese, olive oil, garlic, oregano, salt, and pepper in a large mixing bowl. Place peppers on a baking pan and stuff them with the quinoa mixture. Bake for 30 minutes, or until the peppers are soft.

4. **Mediterranean Veggie Pizza**

**Ingredients include**- pizza dough, olive oil, zucchini, tomatoes, red onion, olives, feta cheese, oregano, garlic, salt, and pepper.

**Preparation**: Heat the oven to 400°F. Place the pizza dough on a baking pan and roll it out. Olive oil should be brushed on. Sliced zucchini, tomatoes, red onion, olives, feta cheese, oregano, garlic, salt, and pepper to taste. Cook for 15-20 minutes, or until the crust is golden brown.

5. **Mediterranean Ratatouille**

**Ingredients include**- eggplant, zucchini, tomatoes, red onion, garlic, olive oil, oregano, thyme, salt, and pepper.

**Preparation**: Heat the oven to 375°F. Make small cubes of eggplant, zucchini, and tomatoes. Toss with chopped red onion, minced garlic, olive oil, oregano, thyme, salt, and pepper on a baking sheet. 30–35 minutes, or until vegetables are soft and gently browned.

6. **Mediterranean Grilled Vegetables**

**Ingredients include**- eggplant, zucchini, red onion, bell peppers, olive oil, garlic, oregano, thyme, salt, and pepper.

**Preparation**: Preheat the grill to medium-high. Make small cubes of eggplant, zucchini, and bell peppers. Toss with chopped red onion, minced garlic, olive oil, oregano, thyme, salt, and pepper on a baking sheet. Grill vegetables until lightly browned and tender, about 10-15 minutes.

**7. Mediterranean Baked Zucchini**

**Ingredients include**- zucchini, olive oil, garlic, oregano, thyme, salt, and pepper.

**Preparation**: Heat the oven to 400°F. Thinly slice the zucchini. Drizzle with olive oil, minced garlic, oregano, thyme, salt, and pepper, and place on a baking sheet. 20-25 minutes, or until golden brown and soft.

## 8.    Mediterranean    Eggplant Parmesan

**Ingredients include**- Eggplant, Olive oil, garlic, Parmesan cheese, breadcrumbs, tomato sauce, oregano, salt, and pepper.

**Preparation**: Heat the oven to 375°F. Cut the eggplant into 12-inch thick rounds. Brush with olive oil, minced garlic, Parmesan cheese, breadcrumbs, tomato sauce, oregano, salt, and pepper on a baking sheet. 30–35 minutes, or until golden brown and soft.

## 9. Mediterranean Stuffed Tomatoes

**Ingredients include**- tomatoes, couscous, artichoke hearts, olives, feta cheese, olive oil, garlic, oregano, salt, and pepper.

**Preparation**: Heat the oven to 375°F. Remove the seeds from the tomatoes and cut them in half. Cook the couscous according to the package directions. Combine cooked couscous, artichoke hearts, olives, feta cheese, olive oil, garlic, oregano, salt, and pepper in a large mixing basin. Place tomatoes on a baking pan and stuff with couscous mixture. Cook for 15-20 minutes, or until the tomatoes are soft.

## 10. **Mediterranean Zucchini Fritters**

**Ingredients include**- zucchini, eggs, breadcrumbs, Parmesan cheese, garlic, oregano, salt, and pepper.

**Preparation**: In a mixing bowl, combine zucchini, eggs, breadcrumbs, Parmesan cheese, minced garlic, oregano, salt, and pepper. Mix until everything is well blended. Melt butter in a nonstick skillet over medium heat. Cook for 2-3 minutes per side, or until golden brown, using a heaping tablespoon of batter.

## 11. **Mediterranean Stuffed Eggplant**

**Ingredients include**- Eggplant, quinoa, artichoke hearts, spinach, feta cheese, olive oil, garlic, oregano, salt, and pepper.

**Preparation**: Heat the oven to 375°F. Scoop out the middle of the eggplant by cutting it in half. Cook the quinoa according to the package directions. Combine cooked quinoa, artichoke hearts, spinach, feta cheese, olive oil, garlic, oregano, salt, and pepper in a large mixing bowl. Place eggplant on a baking pan and stuff it with the quinoa mixture. Bake for 30 minutes, or until the eggplant is soft.

## 12. Mediterranean Chopped Salad

**Ingredients include**: cucumber, tomatoes, red onion, kalamata olives, feta cheese, parsley, olive oil, lemon juice, garlic, oregano, salt, and pepper.

**Preparation**: Prepare the cucumber, tomatoes, red onion, kalamata olives, feta cheese, parsley, olive oil, lemon juice, minced garlic, oregano, salt, and pepper in a large mixing bowl. Place in the refrigerator until ready to serve.

13. **Mediterranean Roasted Eggplant**

**Ingredients include**- eggplant, olive oil, garlic, oregano, thyme, salt, and pepper.

**Preparation**: Heat the oven to 400°F. Thinly slice the eggplant. Drizzle with olive oil, minced garlic, oregano, thyme, salt, and pepper, and place on a baking sheet. Roast the eggplant for

20-25 minutes, or until golden brown and soft.

## 14. **Mediterranean Grilled Zucchini**

**Ingredients include**- Zucchini, olive oil, garlic, oregano, thyme, salt, and pepper.

**Preparation**: Preheat the grill to medium-high heat. Thinly slice the zucchini. Toss with olive oil, minced garlic, oregano, thyme, salt, and pepper on a baking sheet. Grill for 10-15 minutes, or until the meat is gently browned and tender.

## 15. **Mediterranean Ratatouille Stew**

**Ingredients include**- eggplant, zucchini, tomatoes, red onion, garlic, olive oil, oregano, thyme, salt, and pepper.

**Preparation**: In a large pot, heat the olive oil over medium-high heat. Combine the eggplant, zucchini, tomatoes, and red onion in a mixing bowl. Cook for about 5-7 minutes, or until the vegetables are soft. Add the minced garlic, oregano, thyme, salt, and pepper to taste. Simmer for 10-15 minutes, or until vegetables are tender.

# Chapter 6

## Salads

1. **Greek Salad**

**Ingredients include**: Romaine lettuce, tomatoes, cucumbers, red onion, olives, feta cheese, oregano, olive oil, lemon juice, salt, and pepper.

**Preparation**: In a large mixing bowl, combine lettuce, tomatoes, cucumbers, red onion, and olives. Garnish with feta cheese. In a small mixing bowl, combine the olive oil, lemon juice, oregano, salt, and pepper. Toss salad with dressing to mix.

## 2. Mediterranean Chickpea Salad

**Ingredients include**: Chickpeas, tomatoes, red onion, bell peppers, parsley, mint, lemon juice, olive oil, sea salt, and pepper.

**Preparation**: In a large mixing bowl, combine chickpeas. Combine the tomatoes, red onion, bell peppers, parsley, and mint in a mixing bowl. Whisk together lemon juice, olive oil, sea salt, and pepper in a small bowl. Toss salad with dressing to mix.

## 3. Mediterranean Orzo Salad

**Ingredients include**: Orzo, artichoke hearts, tomatoes, olives, feta cheese, parsley, olive oil, lemon juice, garlic, salt, and pepper.

**Preparation**: Make a saucepan of salted water come to a boil. Cook until the orzo is al dente. Rinse with cold water after draining. Place the orzo in a large mixing basin. Combine the artichoke hearts, tomatoes, olives, feta cheese, and parsley in a mixing bowl. In a small mixing bowl, combine the olive oil, lemon juice, garlic, salt, and pepper. Toss salad with dressing to mix.

4. **Mediterranean Quinoa Salad**
**Ingredients include**: Quinoa, cucumbers, tomatoes, red onion, feta cheese, parsley, olive oil, lemon juice, garlic, salt, and pepper.

**Preparation**: Make a saucepan of salted water come to a boil. Cook until the quinoa is al dente. Rinse with cold water after draining. In a large mixing bowl, combine the quinoa. Cucumbers, tomatoes, red onion, feta cheese, and parsley are optional. In a small mixing bowl, combine the olive oil, lemon juice, garlic, salt, and pepper. Toss salad with dressing to mix.

5. **Mediterranean Lentil Salad**

**Ingredients include**: Lentils, tomatoes, red onion, bell peppers, parsley, mint, olive oil, lemon juice, garlic, salt, and pepper.

**Preparation**: Fill a pot halfway with water and add the lentils. Bring to a boil, then reduce to low heat and cook until the lentils are cooked. Rinse with cold water after draining. In a large mixing bowl, combine lentils. Combine the tomatoes, red onion, bell peppers, parsley, and mint in a mixing bowl. In a small mixing bowl, combine the olive oil, lemon juice, garlic, salt, and pepper. Toss salad with dressing to mix.

## 6. Mediterranean Tuna Salad

**Ingredients include**: Tuna, red onions, bell peppers, parsley, mint, olive oil, lemon juice, garlic, salt, and pepper.

**Preparation**: Drain the tuna and set it in a large mixing dish. Combine the red onions, bell peppers, parsley, and mint in a mixing bowl. In a small mixing bowl, combine the olive oil, lemon juice, garlic, salt, and pepper. Toss salad with dressing to mix.

## 7. Mediterranean Avocado Salad

**Ingredients include**: Avocado, tomatoes, cucumbers, red onion, olives, feta cheese, parsley, olive oil, lemon juice, garlic, salt, and pepper.

**Preparation**: Avocado should be peeled and diced. Place in a large mixing basin. Combine the tomatoes, cucumbers, red onion, and olives in a mixing bowl. Garnish with feta cheese. In a small mixing bowl, combine the olive oil, lemon juice, garlic, salt, and pepper. Toss salad with dressing to mix.

## 8. Mediterranean Eggplant Salad

**Ingredients include**: Eggplant, tomatoes, bell peppers, parsley, mint, olive oil, lemon juice, garlic, salt, and pepper.

**Preparation**: Preheat the oven to 375 degrees Fahrenheit. Place the eggplant cubes on a baking pan. Roast for 20 minutes, or until brown and soft, stirring periodically. Put the eggplant in a large mixing bowl. Toss in the tomatoes, bell peppers, parsley, and mint. In a small mixing bowl, combine the olive oil, lemon juice, garlic, salt, and pepper. Toss salad with dressing to mix.

## 9. **Mediterranean Carrot Salad**

**Ingredients include**: Carrots, tomatoes, cucumbers, olives, feta cheese, parsley, olive oil, lemon juice, garlic, salt, and pepper.

**Preparation**: Carrots should be peeled and grated. Place in a large mixing basin. Combine the tomatoes, cucumbers, olives, and feta cheese in a mixing bowl. In a small mixing bowl, combine the olive oil, lemon juice, garlic, salt, and pepper. Toss salad with dressing to mix.

## 10. **Mediterranean Zucchini Salad**

Ingredients include: Zucchini, red onion, bell peppers, parsley, mint, olive oil, lemon juice, garlic, salt, and pepper.

Preparation: Thinly slice the zucchini. Place in a large mixing basin. Combine the red onion, bell peppers, parsley, and mint in a mixing bowl. In a small mixing bowl, combine the olive oil, lemon juice, garlic, salt, and pepper. Toss salad with dressing to mix.

## 11. **Mediterranean Potato Salad**

**Ingredients include**: potatoes, tomatoes, cucumbers, olives, feta cheese, parsley, olive oil, lemon juice, garlic, salt, and pepper.

**Preparation**: Make a saucepan of salted water come to a boil. Cook until the potatoes are soft. Rinse with cold water after draining. In a large mixing bowl, combine the potatoes. Combine the tomatoes, cucumbers, olives, and feta cheese in a mixing bowl. In a small mixing bowl, combine the olive oil, lemon juice, garlic, salt, and pepper. Toss salad with dressing to mix.

## 12. **Mediterranean Fennel Salad**

**Ingredients include**: Fennel, tomatoes, olives, feta cheese, parsley, olive oil, lemon juice, garlic, salt, and pepper.

**Preparation**: Fennel should be trimmed and thinly sliced. Place in a large mixing basin. Toss in the tomatoes, olives, and feta cheese. In a small mixing bowl, combine the olive oil, lemon juice, garlic, salt, and pepper. Toss salad with dressing to mix.

## 13. **Mediterranean Roasted Vegetable Salad**

Ingredients include: Eggplant, zucchini, bell peppers, tomatoes, olives, feta cheese, parsley, olive oil, lemon juice, garlic, salt, and pepper.

**Preparation**: Preheat the oven to 375 degrees Fahrenheit. Place the eggplant and zucchini cubes on a baking sheet. Roast for 20 minutes, or until brown and soft, stirring periodically. In a large mixing dish, combine the roasted veggies. Combine the bell peppers, tomatoes, olives, and feta cheese in a mixing bowl. In a small mixing bowl, combine the olive oil, lemon juice, garlic, salt, and pepper. Toss salad with dressing to mix.

## 14. Mediterranean Spinach Salad

**Ingredients include**: Spinach, tomatoes, cucumbers, olives, feta cheese, parsley, olive oil, lemon juice, garlic, salt, and pepper.

**Preparation**: In a large mixing bowl, combine the spinach. Combine the tomatoes, cucumbers, olives, and feta cheese in a mixing bowl. In a small mixing bowl, combine the olive oil, lemon juice, garlic, salt, and pepper. Toss salad with dressing to mix.

## 15. Mediterranean Beet Salad

**Ingredients include**: Beets, red onion, apples, feta cheese, parsley, olive oil, lemon juice, garlic, salt, and pepper.

**Preparation**: Beets should be peeled and diced. Place in a large mixing basin. Mix in the red onion, apples, and feta cheese. In a small mixing bowl, combine the olive oil, lemon juice, garlic, salt, and pepper. Toss salad with dressing to mix.

# Chapter 7

## Desserts

1. **Greek Yogurt Cheesecake with Honey in the Oven**

**Ingredients include**: 3 cups plain low-fat Greek yogurt, 4 eggs, 1 cup of honey, 2 tbsp. all-purpose flour, 2 teaspoons vanilla extract, and 1/4 teaspoon cinnamon powder

**Preparation**: Preheat the oven to 350 degrees F. (175 degrees C). Grease an 8-inch springform pan with cooking spray. Whisk together the yogurt, eggs, honey, flour, vanilla extract, and cinnamon in a medium mixing dish.

Pour into the springform pan that has been prepared. Bake for 50 minutes in a preheated oven. Allow cooling before serving.

2. **Almond Cake from the Mediterranean**

**Ingredients include**: 2 cups almond flour, 1 tsp salt, 1/2 cup olive oil, Half a cup of honey, 4 eggs, and 1 tsp vanilla extract

**Preparation**: Preheat the oven to 350 degrees F. (175 degrees C). Grease an 8-inch cake pan with cooking spray. In a medium mixing basin, combine the almond flour, baking powder, and salt. In a separate bowl, combine the olive oil, honey, eggs, and vanilla extract. Mix the wet and dry ingredients until well blended. Pour the batter into the prepared cake pan. Cook for 25 minutes, or until a toothpick inserted into the center comes out clean. Allow cooling before serving.

3. **Fruit Tart with Greek Yogurt**

**Ingredients include**: 1/2 cup unsweetened Greek yogurt, 1 teaspoon lemon juice, 2 tablespoons honey, 1/2 teaspoon vanilla extract, 1/2 cup choice fresh fruit, and 1 pre-made 9-inch tart crust

**Preparation**: Preheat the oven to 375 degrees F. (190 degrees C). In a medium mixing dish, combine the yogurt, honey, lemon juice, and vanilla extract. Pour the yogurt mixture into the tart shell. Top with your favorite fresh fruit. Bake for 15 minutes in a preheated oven. Allow cooling before serving.

## 4. Salad of Mediterranean Fruits

**Ingredients include**: 2 cups fresh fruit diced of your choice, 1/4 cup honey 2 tbsp freshly squeezed lemon juice, 2 tablespoons olive oil, 1 teaspoon cinnamon powder, and 1/4 cup walnuts, chopped

**Preparation**: To begin, combine the chopped fruit, honey, lemon juice, olive oil, and cinnamon in a medium mixing dish. Mix until well blended.

Finish with the walnuts. Chill or serve at room temperature.

## 5. **Greek Yogurt Parfait**

Combine the following ingredients: 1 cup Greek yogurt, plain, 1/4 cup honey, 1/2 teaspoon vanilla extract, 1/2 cup fresh berries, and 1/2 cup walnuts, chopped

**Preparation**: In a medium-mixing dish, combine the yogurt, honey, and vanilla extract. In a parfait glass, layer the yogurt mixture with the fresh berries and walnuts. Chill before serving.

6. **Apples Baked with Honey and Cinnamon**

**Ingredients include**: 4 cored and sliced big apples, 1/4 cup honey, 2 tablespoons brown sugar, 1 teaspoon ground cinnamon, and 2 teaspoons melted butter

**Preparation**: Preheat the oven to 375 degrees F. (190 degrees C). Grease an 8-inch baking dish with cooking spray. Place the apples in the baking dish that has been prepared. Combine the honey, brown sugar, and cinnamon in a small mixing dish. Dot the apples with the honey mixture and the butter. Bake for 25 minutes, or until the apples are soft, in a preheated oven. Serve hot.

7. **Melomakarona (Greek Honey Balls)**

**Ingredients include**: 2 cups all-purpose flour, 2 teaspoons baking powder, 1/2 teaspoon cinnamon powder, 1/4 teaspoon nutmeg, ground Half a cup of olive oil, Half a cup of honey, 1/2 cup orange juice, freshly squeezed, 1/4 cup walnuts, chopped, and 1/4 cup almonds, chopped.

**Preparation**: Preheat the oven to 350 degrees F. (175 degrees C). Using parchment paper, line a baking sheet. In a medium mixing bowl, combine the flour, baking powder, cinnamon, and nutmeg. Whisk together the olive oil, honey, and orange juice in a separate bowl. Mix the wet and dry ingredients until well blended. Roll the dough into 1-inch balls and place them on the prepared baking sheet. Flatten slightly. Top with chopped walnuts and almonds. Bake in a preheated oven for 20 minutes. Allow cooling before serving.

**8. Custard with Greek Yogurt**

**Ingredients include:** 2 cups unsweetened Greek yogurt, 2 eggs, 1/4 cup honey, 1 teaspoon vanilla essence, and 1/4 teaspoon cinnamon powder

**Preparation:** Preheat the oven to 350 degrees F. (175 degrees C). Grease an 8-inch baking dish with cooking spray. Whisk together the yogurt, eggs, honey, vanilla extract, and cinnamon in a medium mixing dish. Pour the mixture into the baking dish that has been prepared. Cook for 25 minutes, or until a knife inserted into the center comes out clean. Allow cooling before serving.

## 9. Baklava

**Ingredients include**: half cup chopped walnuts, half cup almonds, chopped, half cup pistachios, chopped, half cup honey, half cup melted butter, half teaspoon cinnamon, and one box thawed phyllo dough.

**Preparation**: Preheat the oven to 350 degrees F. (175 degrees C). Grease an 8-inch baking dish with cooking spray. Combine the walnuts, almonds, pistachios, honey, butter, and cinnamon in a medium mixing bowl. Place aside. Place one sheet of phyllo dough in the prepared baking dish. Brush the pan with melted butter. Brush each layer with melted butter before adding 6 additional sheets of phyllo. Spread the phyllo with the nut mixture. Brush each layer with melted butter before adding 6 additional sheets of phyllo. Bake for 30 minutes in a preheated oven. Allow cooling before serving.

10. **Popsicles with Greek Yogurt and Honey**

**Ingredients include**: two cups unsweetened Greek yogurt, 1/4 cup honey, half teaspoon vanilla essence, and 1/4 teaspoon cinnamon powder

**Preparation**: In a medium-mixing dish, combine the yogurt, honey, vanilla essence, and cinnamon. Fill popsicle molds halfway with the mixture and freeze for at least 4 hours before serving.

11. **Date and Greek Yogurt Bites**

**Ingredients include**: one cup Greek yogurt, plain, one cup chopped dates, 1/4 cup honey, and half cup walnuts, chopped.

**Preparation**: In a medium-mixing dish, combine the yogurt, honey, dates, and walnuts. Scoop the mixture with a teaspoon onto a parchment-lined baking sheet and freeze for 1 hour. Chill before serving.

## 12. Mediterranean Fig Cake

**Ingredients include**: 1 cup all-purpose flour one tsp baking powder, 1/4 teaspoon salt, 1/4 cup olive oil, and 1/4 cup honey, teo eggs, half cup chopped dried figs, and one teaspoon vanilla extract.

**Preparation**: Preheat the oven to 375 degrees F. (190 degrees C). Grease an 8-inch cake pan with cooking spray. In a medium mixing basin, combine the flour, baking powder, and salt. In a separate bowl, combine the olive oil, honey, eggs, and vanilla extract. Mix the wet and dry ingredients until well blended. Fold in the dried figs, if using. Pour the batter into the prepared cake pan. Cook for 25 minutes, or until a toothpick inserted into the center comes out clean. Allow cooling before serving.

## 13. **Orange and Almond Cake from the Mediterranean**

**Ingredients include**: two cups almond flour, half cup olive oil, 1/4 teaspoon salt, Half a cup of honey, four eggs, one tsp vanilla extract, one orange zest, half cup orange juice, freshly squeezed, and 1/4 cup almonds, sliced

**Preparation**: Preheat the oven to 350 degrees F. (175 degrees C). Grease an 8-inch cake pan with cooking spray. In a medium mixing basin, combine the almond flour, baking powder, and salt. Whisk together the olive oil, honey, eggs, vanilla extract, orange zest, and orange juice in a separate bowl. Mix the wet and dry ingredients until well blended. Pour the batter into the prepared cake pan. Sprinkle with the sliced almonds on top. Cook for 25 minutes, or until a toothpick inserted into the center comes out clean. Allow cooling before serving.

## 14. **Greek Yogurt Mousse**

**Ingredients include**: two cups unsweetened Greek yogurt, half cup honey two tbsp freshly squeezed lemon juice, two teaspoons vanilla extract, and 1/4 teaspoon cinnamon powder

**Preparation**: In a medium-mixing dish, combine the yogurt, honey, lemon juice, vanilla essence, and cinnamon. Divide the mixture among individual serving bowls. Allow at least 1 hour before serving to chill.

## 15. **Figs in Chocolate**

**Ingredients include**: 1/4 cup chopped walnuts, half cup chopped dark chocolate, half teaspoon cinnamon powder, and eight figs, fresh

**Preparation:** Place the chocolate in a microwave-safe bowl and microwave for 1 minute on high. Stir until completely melted. Combine the chopped walnuts and cinnamon in a mixing bowl. Each fig should be dipped in the melted chocolate mixture. Place the dipped figs on a baking sheet lined with parchment paper. Allow at least 1 hour before serving to chill.

# Conclusion

The Mediterranean diet is a delightful and highly healthy way to eat. It has been demonstrated to offer several health advantages and is based on the traditional meals of nations like Greece, Italy, and Spain. Fresh, whole foods including fruits, vegetables, legumes, nuts, and whole grains, as well as lean proteins like fish and olive oil, are the main components of the diet.

The diet is not only a scrumptious and nutritious way to eat, but it can also be quite simple and practical. Many of the dishes in this cookbook can be created quickly and easily with items you probably already have in your cupboard. You can quickly prepare healthy meals thanks to the abundance of recipes that can be prepared ahead of time.

Although I am aware that changing one's way of life can be difficult, I hope that this cookbook has been a helpful and pleasant resource. You may take advantage of the many health advantages of the Mediterranean diet by eating a diet high in fresh fruits and vegetables, whole grains, healthy fats, and lean proteins.

Your body will appreciate the nourishing foods you've been consuming and you'll be sure to feel energized and vibrant. So start preparing food now! Enjoy the dishes in this cookbook, and don't be afraid to try out new flavors and ingredients. You'll undoubtedly discover something you love. Bon appetite!